DEFENSES
Getting out of Emotional Prison

Antania M. Barnes

DEFENSES: GETTING OUT OF EMOTIONAL PRISON

Copyright © 2018 Antania M. Barnes

All rights reserved.

ISBN-13: 978-0-692-07486-2
Library of Congress Control Number: 903625
Nia's Relationship & Life Coaching, LLC: Hummelstown, PA

DEDICATION

This book is dedicated to my favorite boys for all the love, patience, and understanding you've shown me. I appreciate all the sacrifices you had to endure while Mommy was learning to be the best mother, Christian, and example for you. I love you, Bryce and Brayden.

CONTENTS

CONTENTS iv
ACKNOWLEDGMENTS v
1 INTRODUCTION 6
2 EMOTIONS AND FEELINGS 10
3 EMOTIONAL BAGGAGE 15
4 TRUTH HEALS 19
5 DISTORTION 23
6 DEFENSE MECHANISMS 30
7 EMOTIONAL PRISON 50
8 HURTING BUT HEALING 57
9 FORGIVENESS 59
10 SKILLS TO HEAL 64
NIA'S STEPS 66
REFERENCES 69

ACKNOWLEDGMENTS

I'd like to take this opportunity to thank my Lord and Savior for giving me the ability to finish this book. I would also like to thank my children, family and true friends. I would also like to thank those of you who were my muse and didn't even know it. I am a better person because of all of you who loved me.

1 INTRODUCTION

I'm sure all of us at some point have felt so down that we couldn't get out of bed or didn't feel like it. We may have felt so down that we couldn't seem to enjoy or participate in normal life activities, whether that be going to work or school, hanging out with friends, going to church, taking care of kids, or tending to a partner's or spouse's needs. The problem is most of us do not realize the power we have over our emotions. We have the capacity to improve our moods but we must learn how so we can get the most out of life. The fact is, we have a natural healing capability that most of us don't even realize we have.

In life there are choices, and the quality of our life depends on the choices we make. We can make our own choices about diet, exercise, sleep, and work, or we can give others the power to control our responses or reactions. Most of our life experiences will be based on the decisions we make. We often fail to realize these decisions have a direct impact on our emotions and state of mind. I don't know how many times I've said, "You are getting on my nerves," or my favorite, "You are messing with my peace." These are words of utter frustration. We all remember those times of failure, and sometimes we regret it because we either acted on that disappointment or only just gave up. The truth is, we all want to live a life that doesn't involve us always being stressed out, depressed, on the defense, or just plain miserable. God didn't promise us a life with no trials or tribulations. He promised that he would always be there and never leave nor forsake us. We suffer because most of us want to live life haphazardly. We want to do the things that provide us with temporary happiness and provide immediate gratification. So, when confronted with difficulty that comes or that we have caused, we utilize our defense mechanisms. However, defenses are not supposed to be used as a permanent armor against pain or difficulties. We suffer because we tell ourselves our lies, view the world from our tainted perceptions, and blame everyone else for our misery. We refuse to live in consistent truth.

Examining oneself can be difficult, because without being aware, you filter your experiences through a tainted lens that allow you to soften truths that prove to be too painful. Researchers and psychologists define this concept as defense mechanisms. Defense mechanisms are described as a mental process initiated, typically unconsciously, to avoid conscious conflict or anxiety. These methods differ in the particular ways in which they function, but they all serve the same purpose, namely, to protect the individual from experiencing excessive anxiety and to protect the self and self-esteem. Different from conscious coping strategies, these mechanisms operate at an unconscious level, so the individual is unaware of how they function.

It has been my experience in working with people, that I have found that the most frequently seen defense mechanisms are: acting out, denial, and rationalization. An example of acting out would be when a person may want to curse and engage in theatrics after smashing a hand in the car door, but the ego, perceiving this as contradicting social etiquette, will often lead them to hold back on the expletives. On some occasions, however, we may not be able to balance the impulses of the id and will defend the ego by merely acting out the irrational desires. For example, a person might "act out" by pouting, giving the silent treatment, or slamming doors after a disagreement when he or she would otherwise stay calm and relax.

The self-denial of one's feelings or previous actions is one defense mechanism to avoid damage to the ego caused by the anxiety or guilt of accepting them. A married man might deny to himself that he likes his wife's friend, rather than allowing his true feelings. People might also deny their physical behavior, such as theft, preferring to think that someone forced them into committing the crime to avoid dealing with the guilt they would feel if they accepted their actions.

Rationalization occurs when people attempt to explain or create excuses for an event or activity in rational terms. In doing so, they can avoid accepting the real cause or reason resulting in the present situation. For example, a woman may abandon her children while giving the excuse that she left them temporarily to take a job that was miles away so that she can provide for them. She rationalizes her absence not realizing the damage she has caused with not being there daily to comfort, nurture, be present at pee wee football games, tuck them in at night, read bedtimes stores, or raise them. However, when she never returns, she tells herself that she was trapped, when the actual cause was her belief that she deserves to live a life free from the burden of having an everyday responsibility of being a parent and raising her children. Another example, would be a man leaving his wife and child with never being a part of his child's life until years later. He makes the excuse that others have made it difficult for him to be a father when the truth is, his selfishness and inability to accept responsibility was the cause. When you rationalize your poor choices, you begin to believe the lies you tell yourself.

As I began to write this book back in 2006—yes, over a decade ago—I wondered what I would focus on. Some years went by. I evolved and as I became a therapist working with families and children dealing with trauma, I became captivated with the process through which people heal. But it wasn't only my experience of working with children and families that piqued my interest but also the trials and tribulations my friends and I went through. Broken hearts, the loss of a child, failed marriages, broken engagements, death, physical abuse, emotional abuse, battling cancer, and dealing with the betrayal of friends led me to become interested in figuring out how, when, and why some people can heal emotionally and mentally while others are still stuck being miserable or being a victim.

The realization of one commonality I discovered while working with clients and listening to friends or even myself is that we all dismissed the truth. Whether it was an adult male, an adult woman, a child, or an adolescent I was working with, they all had to come to the truth and reality of their situation and how they got there. To do this, they had to be honest about what they were feeling. Yes, feelings. No, everything in life won't be "unicorns and rainbows," but learning how to maintain a balance is crucial for living. In the homework assignments I give to my older clients, I always make them journal about what they are feeling and why. I am a firm believer that there is a natural healing process to journaling. It's cathartic. Now, of course, some clients would struggle with identifying how they felt, while others simply would not be honest with themselves. It was no quandary why some did not want to be honest with their feelings, because that meant letting down their defenses and letting the pain inside. It meant being humble.

Examining this from the perspective of a mental-health therapist, I wanted to know how defense mechanisms impact character development and how they block people from knowing and telling their truths and thus interrupting the power to heal emotionally and mentally. Conversely, from a spiritual perspective, it wasn't until I experienced my own significant pain that I realized that only God could heal my wounds. So, after all these years and experiences, I finally realized why I couldn't finish this book until now. God called me not to waste my pain. In this book, I invite you to look within yourself and understand that you hold the power to take the necessary steps toward healing and staying out of "emotional prison." Our natural curing process keeps us well and heals us when we are distressed.

2 EMOTIONS AND FEELINGS

He heals the brokenhearted and binds up their wounds. ~ Psalms 147:3

People wonder what emotional health is, let alone trying to understand how to get it or what it means to them. Emotional health in layman's terms means being able to recognize feelings and having the capability of expressing those good or bad feelings appropriately. Most times, feelings and emotions are used interchangeably. Feelings are mental associations and reactions to an emotion that are personal and acquired through experience. Emotions are event-driven, while feelings are learned behaviors that are hidden until triggered by an external event.

How Emotions Develop

Not too many of us like to talk about feelings and emotions because it usually means placing ourselves in a position of vulnerability. It means allowing ourselves to feel or giving someone else an opportunity to hurt us but also love us. It's a gamble. The secret to knowing who you are and living well begins with understanding the difference between continuous feelings and short-term emotions. Everything you experience in life, no matter how terrible it may be, will never be anything more than a heap of thoughts with the addition of physical sensations. So, ask yourself honestly: Can I handle that? Truthfully, most of us can.

Being able to identify how we are feeling has been shown to reduce the intensity of experience because it reengages our rational minds. The most elegant way to determine the emotion behind a particularly negative feeling is only to ask, "What flabbergasted you?" Name your feelings: anxiety, anger, hurt, disgust, rage or sadness. You can speculate on what you lost that could cause you such a feeling and what might have occurred but you don't need to be sure, you just have to have a suspicion or a clue. However, whatever you discover is ok and do not be discouraged because you think your feelings appear to reflect a person you can't relate to or somebody who you're not proud of. Know that they are your feelings and you are allowed to feel how you feel. It is when you become reluctant to accept these feelings that they become a problem, because when you aren't living in truth, you are operating in defense of denial. If you can't acknowledge your anger, your hurt, or the pain, then you can't understand yourself, and that's the truth. Understanding the underlying cause of why you feel the way you are feeling lies at the heart of self-awareness. If you don't know what hurts you, then how do you know what matters to you? If you don't understand your hurt, then passion remains a mystery to you as well.

You are capable of understanding your feelings because your feelings sendoff little signals, although they're not final verdicts because they can be distorted, confused, exaggerated, or overstated (as they often are)—but know that they are your feelings. Accept your feelings as part of yourself; you don't need to like them, but you do need to be able to identify them and come to terms with them. Understanding your feelings is the catalyst for enlightenment. Furthermore, if you cannot come to terms with how you feel, you won't know if others are mistreating you or if it's you who's projecting your feelings onto someone else. A projection, might I add, is another defense mechanism. I encourage you to get real honest with yourself about how you feel and know that if you conceal the hurt, you will only be setting yourself up for future disappointment.

Accepting Your Part in Old Wounds
The scars we bear lets us know the past was real.

Understanding old feelings proves to be a bit more of a challenge, because for most of us, that means we have to come to terms with some harsh realities. To acknowledge the old feelings means you must be aware of some of your shortcomings and that you're just not so perfect. So when you try to hide these flaws, you become defensive because you have attempted to distort the past and avoid responsibility. Nonetheless, you have to take responsibility for how you responded or how you acted. The fact is, you may have been "on point," or maybe you were immature; maybe sometimes you were fearless, and then sometimes you lied or cheated. If you are emotionally immature, then you will seek to blame others for however you felt. However, before you begin to look at your past, it may be helpful to see the good in you and forgive yourself, because once you start looking at your history, you may discover some negative feelings, thoughts, and actions. You may realize that there were some things you could've handled better or even avoided.

Contrarily, in your mind, you will justify that you had good reasons to respond off of whatever feeling you were feeling. Nevertheless, the reality is that you can't assume that you are innocent and that others were consistently wrong. If you are going to be truthful about your past, you need to accept the fact that you have to take responsibility. It is paramount that you not walk away and have a victim mentality for the things that may have happened to you that you did not like. It is critical that you live in truth and accept responsibility to how you came to be in situations like this because if you do not, you will continue to move on blaming others for your poor choices which will stunt your growth. But in order to accept responsibility, it requires you to be humble. You need to be humble enough to dig deep and figure out why you disregarded your instincts or situations when red flags were all over the place. Was it because you have low self-esteem, was it fear of rejection or something that stems from child-hood? Taking ownership of the things that happened and the role you played in them allows you to gain insight as to how you could handle things in a better manner.

Many will say that they do not like to "dwell on the past" or even think about it—what is done is done. That statement is true in that we cannot turn back the hands of time and get a "do-over." In fact, re-playing the hurt over and over again in your head is like a form of self-abuse. However, one thing is for certain: if you don't have peace about what took place, it will resurface. It will resurface when someone or something triggers you. You may be triggered by something someone says or does, or even a certain smell or place can trigger you. For instance, a woman can experience the heartache of infidelity and tell herself small lies every day that she is "OK." She can tell herself and believe that she deserved better and that ending the marriage was a blessing, all of which may be true. However, if she is angry, each time someone mentions her ex's name or she is reminded of him, subconsciously the pain will resurface. Her responses to that past trauma are what will keep her stuck in her emotional prison.

For example, she could be walking in the mall and a man who wears the same cologne her ex wears well trigger a memory of her ex and the turmoil she experienced. That incident alone could very well end up with her spending the reminder of her day, angry, bitter remembering all the bad things she feels he had done. She may lash out at a friend or colleague, not even realizing that her displaced anger was triggered by something that person said or did that reminded her of her experience. In her mind, she will justify that she had good reasons to feel however she felt. But the reality is that you can't assume that you are innocent and the others were consistently wrong. If you are going to be truthful about your past, you've got to take responsibility. Hiding your hurt only intensifies it. What's done in the dark comes to light, and that light is the truth. Revealing your feelings initiates the healing process.

It Is What It Is

One of the harsh realities of accepting our pasts is that we have to come to terms with the parts that we played in them. I mentioned this earlier because it is necessary in order to move forward. If you look at your history and only see your innocence and that everyone else is the villain, be assured that your mind will allow you to believe just that—but you will not find peace. However, when you decide to heal, you will discover that everything feels better but nothing has changed. In that case, it's you who has turned, and that, my friends, is growth! But let's take it a step further: accept your own "jacked up" way of thinking, recognize the mistakes that you made in life, realize you were selfish, and admit that you were once hurtful or jealous or however you were. Those are harsh realities because it means you can't avoid taking responsibility for hurting others, even if you justify it as self-righteous retaliation for getting back at someone who hurt you. It means you can't leave out the part where you may have messed up and made mistakes too. The damage you do when you have a sense of arrogance or entitlement to retaliate supersedes anything you cause through negligence. It's about healing and being emotionally healthy. The natural healing process is inside each of us. There is a therapeutic process that serves to keep you open and emotionally free, but when the lies you tell yourself block the healing process, avoiding the truth results in a failed healing process, and you remain stuck with emotional baggage.

3 EMOTIONAL BAGGAGE

How can we rid ourselves of it?

Identifying Emotional Scars

To identify emotional scars, we need to determine the problem and realize the need for inner healing. If you don't want to heal and move forward in life, you won't. If you do, then you will take the necessary steps to do so. However, some of us may not even realize that we have these scars because we are unable to identify them. We are unable to identify how they are showing up in our lives. Both personal and professional experiences have afforded me the opportunity to know emotional baggage. I am reminded of the famous singer Erykah Badu's song "Bag Lady." Ms. Badu belts out a melodic tune urging women to let go of all of their emotional baggage. While the theme was like an anthem for women's healing, there is no doubt the sentiment (can relate to men too). When your heart has been broken, and you don't deal with it, you will develop emotional baggage. If you don't let it out, you will act it out in very unhealthy ways.

Emotional pain is very much like going through grief. If you don't grieve over your hurt and go through the process, you will spend the remainder of your life reacting and taking it out on other people around you or on your own body. Below is a list of some of the emotional baggage that most of us don't even realize we are carrying. Some are familiar symptoms to look for in yourself or someone else in your life. While the list isn't exhaustive, it can certainly open your eyes to what emotional baggage looks like. Remember to keep an open mind and be truthful.

Avoidance: The internal tempest that occurs that makes it easy for one to escape or suppress reality. So what does this look like? Avoidance can show up in the form of drinking, smoking, having multiple partners, promiscuity, overeating, porn, gambling. When people try to escape from their reality, addictions can form, which makes the habits virtually impossible to break.

The Belief That You're Unworthy of Love: It is hard to see and realize the respect of others and God in your life. An example of this could be people who self-sabotage in relationships. These people could know that they have the right partner, but their crippling fear of rejection and low self-esteem leads them to destroy their relationships.

Depression: Feelings of hopelessness and pain from current or unresolved issues make it difficult to see how anyone can love or care for you, especially God, because you have blocked him out. When he is not the center of your life, or you do not have a relationship, it becomes hard to see how God loves and cares for you, so you develop hopelessness.

Becoming Easily Annoyed: Because of inner turmoil that is caused by a hidden wound, it is easy to become quickly frustrated with ordinary people in your life and daily responsibilities. This pollutes the atmosphere around you, and it brings your emotions down. When you are irritable, anyone and anything can bother you.

Feelings of Anger toward God: When a person is struggling and going through trials and tribulations that have caused them tremendous pain, it's easy to place blame on God and ask, "How did God let this happen?" With this mind-set, you don't seek to be healed, and you develop a wall. For believers, please understand one thing: only God can heal the matters of the heart, but he will not override your free will. If you hold hatred in your heart, that is not of God, and it prevents you from any progress.

Lashing Out: When there's an inner wound that has festered and has come to the place where it may explode, you will see lashing out. Lashing out looks like bouts of anger, rage, or even resentment. Be careful, because you may find it easy to lash out at people who love you and who have done you no harm.

Perfectionism: Some of us need to be perfect. It stems from unmet needs growing up and the need for attention. It could even stem from an emotional wound. It leads you to the mind-set of always trying to please other people, prove yourself, and seek validation.

Self-Hate: Many times when people feel hurt from past abuse, they think that what happened to them was their fault and they somehow deserved it. They also start to believe they are not worthy of love. Always remember that it is not OK to abuse anyone or allow yourself to be abused emotionally, mentally, or physically.

Self-Harming: A person who is a cutter usually has a lot of pain inside, and a way to release it is through cutting.

Unforgiveness: This keeps you in emotional jail, and it inhibits your ability to develop emotionally. Unforgiveness ages you and wreaks havoc in your mind and body because you remain consumed by the offense someone committed against you instead of forgiving them.

Vindictiveness: This is stored anger and resentment because of unforgiveness. It festers like cancer, eating away at you to the point where you become toxic. When you are vindictive, you will stop at nothing to "pay others back" for their offenses against you.

Zero Tolerance: There is a low tolerance for others, where you expect and demand from them. Conversely, having zero tolerance for people and their shenanigans is acceptable. For example, if your ex- partner is playing with your emotions and says that he or she wants the two of you to get back together but their behavior says otherwise, then its ok to have zero tolerance for their bullcrap.

DEFENSES: GETTING OUT OF EMOTIONAL PRISON

Now I want you to take a moment and think about the list. Although not exhaustive, it provides an opportunity for you to examine the things that you may need to heal and let go of. You need to say to yourself, its time to let go and its ok to let go. I am not suggesting that you just "get over it" because that is dismissive and non-validating. No one is saying that your feelings cannot be validated or that you don't have a right to feel hurt, angry, sad or frustrated but what you cannot do is remain in that state for a lifetime and expect to live a life that is fruitful and stress free. I hope that in dealing with your truth, you can begin to take the necessary actions to move forward in life.

4 TRUTH HEALS

I have no greater joy than to hear that my children walk in truth.
~ 3 John 1:4

As I reflect on my career as a therapist helping clients deal with depression, life stressors, and disappointments, the one thing that remained consistent was the need to face the truth about things. Even as I reflected on my trials and tribulations, I realized that I needed to deal with the truth. Often, we distort the truth because it doesn't feel right. Let's face it, no one would knowingly gravitate toward things that are unpleasant for them. In any epiphany that occurred, at that moment, it was coming to terms with what was true that finally allowed for the healing to commence.

As a counselor, I often equated it to being like a personal trainer of feelings. When you are training someone, in that first session you get a truthful assessment of where he or she is physically and help set and achieve realistic goals. As that person progresses, his or her overall well-being improves. With emotions, it makes sense to try to figure out if you can identify the event that caused your feelings, placing the emotion into perspective. It doesn't matter how difficult or confusing the situation may be, putting it in the simplest terms makes the difference. When you lose a loved one, it is the truthful acceptance of that hurtful loss that initiates the grief process, but it eventually leads to some relief.

Similarly, the goal of a couple in therapy is to get each partner to reveal how they feel about each other. No significant gains can be made until both partners arrive at the same level of commitment and understanding, but more than anything, whether the marriage fails or succeeds depends on how much the truth the partners can tell or hear from each other. It is only when couples express their true feelings—no matter how unpleasant or ugly—that the relationship can be on the road to healing.

Many people struggle with depression and don't want to admit it because to them, mental-health problems are taboo or only for people who are "crazy." This is a lie that they came to believe while not dealing with their truth. The symptoms of depression are likely to be compounded if not dealt with healthily. Anxiety, loneliness, and anger erode you; then on another day, anger shows up. The anger can be about multiple causes. You can become angry at your friends, family, a particular situation, or even a simple statement or comment. These wavelengths will be likely to continue, much like depression and anxiety, which come in wavelengths or coincide. The importance of being truthful has everything to do with understanding that your concealment of feelings is only serving to exacerbate your depression or whatever woes you may be experiencing.

Both professionally and personally, it became very clear to me that resolving most of life's difficulties requires telling or hearing the truth that no one wants to hear. For example, when a friendship goes south, it is usually because there was a misunderstanding or distortion of facts. Even so, in broken relationships, what the other person wants—or at least one of them is hoping for—is that there's a chance to air out the truth and set matters straight. Truth has the power to heal and to protect. Living in truth is always best.

Let's explore this little thing about the truth even further. Concealing lies is so draining it's ridiculous. It zaps you of your strength, and it drains you of your energy because you always have to be thinking of lies to tell yourself or someone else. The truth of the matter is that when people live in a lie, they invite more trouble into their lives rather than making them better. Both personally and professionally I wondered about living in truth and its natural healing power. I recall some therapy sessions with a client where when I would recap what was said in the previous sessions, some of my clients became bothered by what they had said. They would question themselves and ask, "Did I say that?" Similarly, have you ever had the experience of someone telling you that you said something and you began to question yourself because you probably needed to put yourself in "time-out"?

In that regard, what seems to bother us the most is the fact that we don't like to hear the truth about some things because it's ugly. When you uncover the lies you tell yourself, you discover deception, and in a sense, you begin to heal. This is a healing process that many don't even realize. But it is a defense mechanism that people use to block out some painful or unpleasant feelings. As I explored defense mechanisms as they relate to healing, I discovered that we either blame someone for our problems, tell bald-faced lies to ourselves by denying our problems, or we make crappy excuses.

Denial: Our Strongest Defense

Denial is a potent defense. It prevents hurt from intruding into your awareness. It shuts off perception when it is dangerous, only opening it when it's safe. Denial is not black and white; there's a gray area because, at times, the truth does seep through. Quite often, you turn away from what hurts and force yourself to forget it's there without defining what it is you're shutting out. Even so, you expect that something wrong exists, and you hope it will be gone when you open your eyes. For example, you go through denial when you lose someone. Sometimes you are stunned, shocked, and don't want to believe that it is true. I remember an ex telling me a story about how he and his best friend almost died in battle during the war. At that moment, I am sure he blocked out his fear when going into the fight but was still aware of what was happening. Denial could be high or low, but it is necessary to lower your denial to permit some painful truth to enter your awareness so that you can initiate healing. If you are unsure of what denial looks like, here are some forms: hoping, sidetracking, lying, misplacing, not seeing or hearing, and the list goes on.

Let's focus on a few so we can move on. The concept of hope and denial starts with wishing; you are hoping that the truth isn't the truth and you will be rescued. But some continue to hope when all hope is gone. In sidetracking, you divert others to prevent them from looking at the same evidence you're trying to avoid. Many others don't share your point of view, so when they state the truth they validate your worst fears. Truthfully, when you are sidetracking, it suggests that you are aware of the thing you're trying to deny. With lying, you lie to yourself and others to hide the truth. Regardless of what form of denial takes, it keeps you trapped.

5 DISTORTION

Defenses

The purpose of your defenses is to cushion you from all the impact of fear and hurt so that you can try to function. Your defenses are designed to provide a temporary fix and alert you to danger or loss. The way you use your defenses provides a template for how you screen your pain. It also sets the tone for your style of coping. Your defenses give you a view of the world, and as you become in a choke hold with them, your defense pattern becomes your reality. You're distorted from truth. However, it is only when you admit the truth of your pain that healing commences. You cannot get better if you refuse to feel, and you cannot grow if you are always on the defense. Let me repeat that: you cannot improve if you are always on the defense.

A Temporary Fix

Defenses allow you to live in a fantasy world because they shield you from pain, but it's only temporary. In a make-believe world that you concoct, you get to have everything your heart desires, and you get to have everything you've ever wanted by any means. But the truth is, that is not reality. The fact of the matter is that when you live in your lies or in a make-believe world, the heavy price you pay is that you are losing the ability to take risks, sincerely and genuinely love and be loved, or be happy. The problem is that you don't like anything that tells the truth or you avoid it like the plague because it is often difficult to experience reality. Unfortunately, you then become a prisoner to your defenses. While more than half of the people of the world utilizes defenses to survive, it doesn't allow us to avoid pain. You don't get off the hook that easy. While you may not be able to prevent pain, and suffering no matter what defense you employ, if you use defenses the way they should be used, they can provide a buffer until you can "get it together" and respond accordingly. The bottom line is this: if you apply the same logic, it is only going to yield the same results.

You Still Haven't Learned

Many of us don't want to look at our faults and will fight against anyone who points them out because it threatens our self-image we have of ourselves. Some of us who haven't evolved even become angered and will dismiss anyone who points out our wrongdoings. Many of us don't want to take responsibility for actions or admit that we are in trouble, and the defense mechanisms we employ hide our faults from our awareness. When something goes wrong, your defenses are on "high alert" or "overdrive" for you to protect yourself from what's happening. You have to use your defenses even more to shield you from the reality of the problems you caused yourself. The problem lies in the fact that it shouldn't take something extraordinary to get your attention or for you to mess up so significantly that you almost can't recover. The sad part about it is that when things like this happen because you are so accustomed to telling yourself your own lies, you're stunned, you're shocked. You even pretend to be flabbergasted, yet you have to admit that it is happening. While you are surprised this issue has caught you off guard as well as you thought this could never happen, you aren't prepared to deal with it because you never took it seriously. So now you must admit your perception was tainted, as was your reasoning, so your self-esteem goes to poop. Your self-esteem dwindles because you begin to internalize whatever mishap that has occurred and allow it to define who you see yourself as rather than acknowledging that you made poor choices or decisions. Now you are sitting there twiddling your thumbs and all the criticism you pushed away comes back to haunt you. You begin to question if you were ever right, yet the *collapse of the defensive* wall provides the view you needed in order to find the right way. Sadly, some people just keep on raising their defense walls and continue to hide. Never learning, never growing. Let's look at a picture of what this looks like.

This explains why people have repeated maladaptive behaviors or patterns of abusive behavior. For instance, in relationships you're still going to date the same guy who is a Ferrari with a Pinto engine; you're always going to chase after the same lame women, play "captain save em'." For those of you who are not familiar with these vernaculars, let me clarify. Dating the guy who is the Ferrari with the Pinto engine means he looks good on the outside but his inside is ugly. He presents well, maybe he's even well spoken, but when he shows his true colors, you realize he is a fraud and his inside isn't so attractive. He is emotionally immature, bitter, doesn't know how to show love, and functions in unbridled selfishness—and trying to maintain a relationship with him means you poison yourself.

Playing "captain save em' " is for the guy who doesn't admit to himself he has low self-esteem, so he tends to go after women who will stroked his ego because he needs to feel wanted and his self-worth is measured by how many praises and accolades he receives. It can also be measured by how many women he gets. This is the guy who only wants to hear how great he is and if you call him on his bullcrap, he will dismiss you, despise you and cut you off because in his mind you threaten "his false sense" of self-esteem. In his quest to save the day, he seeks out women who are hurt and wounded in order to play like a mentor to them. Although he tells himself he is slick, behind his facade is a guy who is insecure. His yearning to rescue the damsel in distress is rooted in his fear of rejection.

The "captain save em'" women tend to use these type of men unknowingly to them because they are so caught up in getting their ego stroked, they fail to realize when they are being used and or manipulated. He thinks he is coming in to save the day with his cape but he doesn't realize behind that outer appearance, this kind of woman is very cunning and conniving. When I think about these situations I recall Proverbs 7: 21-23. Often times he is so blinded by lust and his need to boost his self-esteem that he doesn't realize when this type of female is done with him, he will have lost just about everything. These women typically lack sound values, have low self-esteem themselves, need to be the center of attention, have a million selfies on social media that are typically inappropriate, are highly sexualized, promiscuous, have been through a cycle of some form of abuse and want someone to pay all their bills and take care of them; they use their bodies and manipulation to get what they want from this type of man. They operate with a Jezebel spirit. I hope that clarifies.

    I used the example of relationships because relationships are so important and you have relationships with everyone. You have romantic relationships, business relationship, family relationships, friendships, relationships with members in your church, school, jobs etc. However, not every relationship you have will be fruitful. Some relationships are toxic and you will still hang onto them even though they are poisoning your system. You may have gotten rid of Rick who was the Ferrari with the Pinto engine but you moved on to Darren who was another Ferrari with a Pinto engine. You may have gotten rid of Tonya who was loose and no good for you but you moved on to Kim who was the same. So there you are, failed relationship after failed relationship because they have no substance. After all how could they when you haven't dealt with your own issues within yourself? The faces may have changed but you keep running into the same type of people because you're approach is still the same and you haven't learned. Remember bad company corrupts good character. Choose wisely because often times, the people you deal with are helping you remain stuck. Stuck in repeating the same patterns of behavior that hasn't added to your life and stuck in your ways of thinking and along with how you deal with things.

    So, when you haven't learned, you still hang around the same friends who have no life goals and are lazy; you are still content with mediocrity, you stay with people who are negative, you still use your body to get attention, when you have multiple babies and do not raise them, when you sow a negative seed and then are perplexed as to how things come back on you, when you quit job after job, when you don't take care of your own kid(s) but rather someone else's depending on what woman your dealing with for the season, when you are looking for someone to complete you, when you chase after a man but neglect your kids, when you are looking for a guy to take care of you, when you keep on being the "side piece", when you have failed relationship after failed relationship, when you go from church to church because the pastor at each church isn't preaching to your liking, when you move to a new parish, you don't like the priest or parishioners and when you remain stuck in the same miserable job, you have yet to learn your lesson! Newsflash, the common denominator is you. The scary part of this is that you begin to believe this false notion that the world is against you, but the reality is that you still haven't learned.

Nature versus Nurture:
Family Influence Shapes Our Defenses

The old nature-nurture debate comes to mind when we talk about our character and how the defenses we use affect our lives. Honestly, children from the same parents and same upbringing adapt to the world around them differently and often have distinctly different personalities. Working in both child welfare and the mental-health fields has afforded me the opportunity to witness what I call "generational messed-upness." From a spiritual perspective, we call those "generational curses."

While working with kids and families, I have often wondered if the parents didn't have all these issues, then maybe the child wouldn't have these behavioral and emotional problems. A lot of times their issues stems from the environment they were being raised in. As I pondered on how the family circumstances shaped their development, it was not hard to believe they shaped their defense mechanisms too. Not only were their defense mechanisms shaped by their families, but also their character. Their defense patterns were shaped by how they had to react to their family situations. It was the effects of these patterns that didn't allow these kids to openly express their feelings, thus creating what I call "emotional baggage" that started early on.

From a family systems perspective, it was clear to see how children are coerced and bullied by situations that are so commonplace to them that they don't even realize them as hurtful or damaging. Instead, when they "go against the grain" (because they feel differently from everyone's expectations), they start to question themselves. This begins the thought that they are outsiders, and now they begin to questions their own ability to make judgments. This self-doubt hinders their openness to feel, and so they develop emotional debt following their family's pattern of defensive rules.

Examples of Defense Patterns

In child welfare, I have worked with families where one or both the parents were addicted to drugs. These kids on my caseload had to grow up fast and typically suffered from constant anxiety based on the fact that they did not know what they would endure when they got home—if there even was a home to go to. They never knew if they would have food, shelter, or comfort, or be met with yelling and screaming and angry outbursts. Children living in these conditions develop feelings of shame, embarrassment, and often internalized anger from dealing with their family circumstances, which later turns into issues with low self-esteem. I recall one case where I watched the child go from childhood all the way through young adulthood. I remember when working with him earlier on that the child would always, without fail, make excuses for his parents' behavior. Regarding defenses, the kids in this situation didn't manage their emotional debts efficiently, but how could they? They had no examples. However, the problem lies in the fact that it manifests itself as criticism or projection. Later in life, they become attracted to addicts as a way of working out their stored anger toward a parent.

It is important to note how your family shaped your defensive style because it helps you gain insight into your ability to distort things. The manner in which your family encouraged you to tell untruths becomes your emotional defense heritage. It is not until you recognize the patterns of dysfunction or emotional camouflage that you will be able to rid yourself of repeating the same patterns and being stuck in emotional debt.

However, the journey of self-discovery initiates with having a keen understanding of how we grew up. This would require asking yourself questions and reflecting on the answers. "How was I raised?" "What strengths did it give me?" "What weaknesses did I get?" Our families provide a framework of unspoken rules to live by. Nevertheless, we learn from what we saw growing up. There are not many of us who are surprised when we witness a young girl who watches her mom chase after abusive men grow up to desire the same type of man. We all have said we will never be like our parents, but the truth is that sometimes we adopt some of those same characteristics. I used this example to share that you too may be aware of harmful patterns of learned behaviors, but without first acknowledging them and getting help it is difficult to free yourself from self-destructive behaviors. You tell yourself that it's your reality when it's a lie.

On the contrary, there is nothing that is set in stone to say that because you grew up one way, you will automatically become that very thing that you despise. No, I am not asserting that at all, but what I am saying is that those experiences shaped you to some degree whether it was for you to say to yourself, "I will never be like this; I will do this instead," or, "I can understand why I think and act this way; it's my normal."

6 DEFENSE MECHANISMS

Take down ungodly walls you use to protect you. You can do ALL things through Christ who strengthens you. ~Phillipians 4:13

Defenses Mechanisms: Parts of Your Character

To recap, defense mechanisms are processes in the brain that make an individual forget or ignore painful or disturbing thoughts, situations, or actions. They are a reaction in one's body that protects against disease or danger, and an often-unconscious mental process (oppression) that makes possible solutions to personal problems. Now that defense mechanisms are defined, you are probably wondering whether or not you use them on a regular or daily basis. If you think back to every time you faced an unpleasant circumstance or person, then you can imagine that you deployed some defense mechanism. Conversely, it should be noted that defense mechanisms are not necessarily all bad.

Your defenses are an essential part of your character because they inform you as to how both positive and negative experiences shape your life. Your defenses are in direct correlation to how you illustrate how genuine, forgiving, compassionate, loving, and trusting you are. Interestingly enough, they can also facilitate how deceitful, distrusting, resentful, dishonest, and spineless you are. If you are rigid in your defenses, you compromise your self-esteem, which can lead to self-destruction. Real talk: your defenses can make you blind, deaf, and dense. When you are so caught up in using your defenses, you are so guarded, fearful, and mistrustful—which in turns inhibits your ability to grow.

Vulnerability creates a lot of angst for most people because it means you have to let your guard down and lower your defenses. However, when you are willing to drop your defenses, you can then begin to learn from your experiences and decide to "keep it moving." It takes a while to learn that vulnerability doesn't necessarily equate to not using your defenses, but rather you can now make informed decisions about when to use them. It means you can accept yourself and your imperfections. And so, the moment you decide not to hide behind your defense mechanisms is when you can be able to receive something such as "constructive criticism" without lashing out or becoming ridiculously defensive. You can even handle disappointment without feeling your world is going to end. Let me take it a step further: when you are not so defensive, you can manage your mishaps and understand how you contributed to them.

In life, you will experience many joys and many pains. God didn't promise you a life without trials and tribulations, but he said that he'd never leave you nor forsake you (Deut. 31:8). It's about growth and living a life of emotional, mental, and physical health. Without change, there is no growth. Without change, there is no loss—and no loss is without some form of pain. However, healing is what is essential, and your character determines the way that you address the healing process.

Your character type includes both positive and negative qualities as well as your defense patterns. Even if you are an individual with "your stuff together," you still use defense mechanisms when faced with stressors. The difference is that when you are emotionally mature, you confront your problems and do not run. Instead, you cope with them and release your defenses. You choose to deal in truth and reality as opposed to avoidance. Personal growth comes from the framework that even though your character was shaped by negative things that happened, it also experienced positivity as well. Personal growth allows for enhancement in all areas of a person's life so they can live a satisfying and productive life. When you resolve your problems and release emotional debt, you are no longer limited by your defenses, and you can view the world from another perspective that isn't hindered by always using them.

Your personality represents your defensive mode, determining both how you deal with pain and what you accept as reality. Each person has a concoction of defenses he or she utilizes, but in effort to explain how defense mechanisms can negatively affect a person's life, I will describe three unique defense characters: controlling, needy, and cutthroat. You can have a blend of all three. To give life to how defense patterns affect your character, I have endeavored to explain those three by applying them to characters: Lamar, Shannon, and Leroy.

The Wolf in Sheep's Clothing (Controlling)
Lamar

Lamar was the third child and often described himself as a good kid who everyone loved and adored. His parents divorced; he remained close to his father, and his father raised him. Lamar became estranged from his mother because when his parents divorced she left the kids with his dad and ran off to live her own life. As an adult, he described his relationship with his mother as abandonment. He didn't realize that trauma from that experience shaped the way he dealt with interpersonal relationships.

He described his romantic relationships as always needing to have his way and using manipulation at times to get it. His philosophy was "better you get hurt than me." It's not surprising he became that way to have the power to protect himself from abandonment and to avoid feeling vulnerable. Being well liked and popular was vital to him. He always had to be viewed as smart, right, and reliable to the point where he appeared to be very narcissistic. He would admittedly say that he cares little for other people's feelings. His defense mechanism was merely to place blame on others when it was discovered he was not right. He was bright in using his control to dismiss his feelings of helplessness and to keep others from rejecting him. Let's break this down.

The Wolf in Sheep's clothing
Borders

In a sense, setting up and maintaining boundaries is a controlling person's road map to how they interact in life. Lamar drew barriers between himself and his feelings, seeking to isolate himself from any emotion that might make him look weak. He never accepted responsibility for his difficulties, nor could he come to terms with them. He was emotionally immature and manipulative. Nothing was ever his fault but rather everyone else's; with that, he could establish boundaries and the rationalizations for keeping them in place. However, in the process of creating his barriers, they were often so severe that he isolated himself from others. This leads controlling people to suffer from loneliness whether they enjoy being alone or not. This is when you will see them seek out pleasure in other ways. They may go out drinking, join a dating site, text an old lover, or do whatever they can to deal with the loneliness. But whatever they do, it will be on their terms, to have as much control as possible.

In Lamar's case, although he isolated himself at times, he liked being around like-minded people if he had to socialize, and this was because his thoughts were in direct contrast to most. He had his own reality, and people existed in "his" world. Most of the time he struggled to take on someone else's point of view and lacked empathy. He seldom ever admitted he was wrong, and if he did, it was only in an attempt to avoid some form of rejection.

The Wolf in Sheep's clothing
He's Correct

Being correct or being seen as superior is of the utmost importance to the controlling defense character. Lamar was the witness, jury, judge, executioner, jailer, and the prosecutor. In the case of Lamar, in his perverse way, he was also the preacher listening to confessions and testimonies and granting forgiveness. He maintained that his right actions, right choices, his right thinking, and proper plotting could never hurt another person. He may have acted without others' agreement, but never with the intention of actually doing anyone harm.

However, this absolute belief in his rightness, combined with his total exercise of power, did a lot of damage. Lamar tended to hurt those who were dependent on him because he knew he had all the control. His controlling patterns of abuse were subtle, well thought out, planned, and challenging for a needy/dependent person to fight because they were disguised by the appearance of him giving. One of the most complicated things a controlling person must face is that, despite the fact they can prove they're conclusively right, they are often wrong. Lamar hated to hear this and would try to argue his point until other people agreed with him. However, when they didn't, he would become enraged. You see, coming to terms with the fact that he wasn't always correct in his thinking revealed his imperfections. This was frightening because his logic was the foundation of his inner rationalizations, the way he relieved himself from guilt and blame. Lamar couldn't come to terms with the fact that his thinking was illogical because that was what he equated his self-esteem to. Therefore, if his thoughts are erroneous, then that must mean something was wrong with him.

The Wolf in Sheep's clothing
Critique

The controlling person tends to criticize, although it's always disguised as critiquing or positive feedback. After all, they are just trying to help you out so you can be better. And if you're a naïve person who believes everyone is innately good you'll be blindsided by their slyness. In all actuality, they have low self-esteem. They project their self-criticism onto others. The only time the controlling person is willing to admit to criticism is after being rejected. But watch out, because his admittance to his faults is only done so reluctantly and the promises that he makes to change will not last. Occasionally, whatever deep hurt he experienced may allow him to grow, but often when the other person shows forgiveness and returns, his resolve shifts from correcting his faults to keeping the other person under control and preventing future abandonment. He will do anything to regain his power back in the situation or relationship. He takes criticism badly and never forgets or forgives it, especially if it is done in public. If you're the person who has criticized him in public, watch out, because it will be his mission to pay you back. He perceives revealing his imperfections as a weakening of his control, and he has this silly belief that he's being set up to be clowned or ridiculed. In the example of Lamar, he found it second nature to criticize others. Even though he did this, he viewed it as necessary, helpful, and instructive; it was an act that was done out of love. Let's be clear as to what the above statement is conveying: a disguised form of criticism is his tendency to comment on everything anyone says or does or appears to be thinking. He is an expert on movies, a critic for food, an expert driver, singer, encyclopedia, and fitness instructor. He knows the right way to do everything!

The Wolf in Sheep's clothing
Anxiety

The controlling person is always fearful of losing power. He is interested in gaining as much of information as he can before he makes a decision. The need to be sure can paralyze him. Losing control is a constant struggle with him, and since he believes his ways are right, he usually seeks out consultants who validate his point of view. What he wants most is someone to agree that he is right in making the decision he has already decided upon so he can act on it with assurance and feel good about himself since he genuinely suffers from low self-esteem. It just reaffirms the lies he tells himself that everyone thinks as he does. He becomes defensive when he is questioned about anything, and it is in such moments that he is likely to increase high risk taking just to demonstrate that he's confident in what he's doing. He foolishly goes against the grain trying to prove himself, but in reality, his impulsivity causes him to lose just about everything. Sometimes he completely abandons all known common sense by following "his rules" to the letter, even when they no longer apply. This kind of "donkeyness" has been responsible for him ruining relationships, whether it be friendships, romantic relationships, or work relationships by being fired.

The Wolf in Sheep's clothing
Rejection

Rejecting a controlling person could be seen as a death sentence because, in a sense, that person is not likely to forget it. He or she will view the person doing the rejecting as being ungrateful. The controlling person will be slow to forgive—if he or she truly ever does—and make every attempt to feel vindicated by getting back at the person who rejected them. For example, a woman client who had been in an abusive relationship with a guy had finally broken free and become independent. She had been planning her escape for a while. But her leaving made him enraged and resentful, and he believed that she did not appreciate him. Of course, it wasn't that she hadn't appreciated whatever he did for her, but she was tired of the abuse and decided to finally leave. In this example, the controlling person could either continue to become angry or grow. You see, for the controlling defense character, this could be a pivotal moment because he has the chance to admit that he actually does need other people. He could accept his vulnerability; however, it is only when he concedes to this that he will begin to see the light. He will see how he lost everything to start with because he really had a fear of losing, and then he'll understand that everybody wants to be wanted but not be possessed.

The Wolf in Sheep's clothing
Four-Letter Word: Love

Let's go back to Lamar, shall we? Lamar had significant difficulty showing or receiving love. This stemmed from some childhood rejection, which resulted in his low self-esteem. He grew up in a household where his family was not very affectionate. The critical thing with controlling people who have difficulty showing love or saying they love you is that if they do those things, it's a little bit too much like surrendering to unconditional love when they were brought up on conditional love.

To further explain, it means that they only received love contingent upon them acting right, doing something pleasing, or as long as they don't step outside the box. Let me break it down a little further. You see, Lamar's ability to love freely depends on the ability to say "you hurt me," and if one cannot express hurt between lovers, love quickly fades behind the stored resentment. This can be especially problematic for a controlling person. Lamar was reluctant to admit that other people hurt him unless he was trying to make them feel guilty, manipulate them into doing whatever he wanted them to do, or use and abuse them in some way. In his mind, if he admitted to others that they hurt him, he realized that he could be hurt and he'd be showing them how they could get back at him. Authentically and unselfishly showing love to a person meant that he had to be vulnerable, and being vulnerable indicated that he was going to lose some form of power.

Conversely, for the controlling person character types, there are times that they truly just do not know how or what love is. He wants to be loved on his terms; he wants it when he wants it, and that's the end of it. He expects the other person to love him according to his needs and whines about the other person needing to know his needs. Often, you'll see that sex becomes a ritual to these people; when it is denied, they will begin to pout and behave as though it is an unforgivable act. It is that unforgivable act that leads to them cheating and having partners on the side or destroying their relationship. Be wary of the wolf in sheep's clothing.

Positive Attributes of the Controlling Person

Although there are probably some challenging things about controlling people, let's not get it twisted. The world wouldn't function without someone willing to be in control and take the lead. After all, the world needs leaders and people who won't just stand still and not make moves. We need "movers and shakers". If you think about it, the controlling character is the "meat and potatoes" of our government, defense department, justice system, and so on. They are managers, facilitators, and organizers ensuring that things run correctly and get done.

Just think of it this way: What if the controlling person is the doctor whose innovative ways save the lives of many? The way the world works, everything bought, traded, delivered, or sold needed a person who was in control to arrange it and make it happen.

When the controlling person has developed and is willing to be vulnerable, he is the supportive person everyone needs. He is the person who is reliable and dependable. He is the person who can compromise and take on someone else's point of view. Although the list of positive qualities of the controlling types is short in comparison to the previous pages discussed, make no mistake about it—there is value in the controlling character.

The "Needy" Person
Shannon

Shannon was an only child, since her younger sister died at birth. She was raised in a single-parent household where her mother resented her for ruining her life. Shannon would often describe her bond with her mother as a love-hate relationship. She endured emotional, physical, and verbal abuse from her mother. She got called foul names and would have to fend off her mother's unprovoked violent attacks. Shannon seemed always to be concerned with being loveable and caring for her friends and family. She still needed to be well liked. Her friends would describe her as nurturing, a people pleaser and a sweetheart. She held the belief that if she was lovable, then others would love her, protect her, and provide for her needs. She is what I consider the dependent/needy person. She grew up in a house that was unloving, and it was no surprise that she would always choose men who were unloving in hopes of one day winning them over. Failed relationships made her question her lovability, but interestingly enough she didn't recognize that she always chose a controlling mate.

You see, the controlling partner didn't give her all she needed or wanted, because then he would be giving away too much. He had to hold something back to keep her depending on him. Take Shannon, for example; she was so in love with this guy that she felt guilty for wanting love and affection, although her mate would not give it. She recognized that she needed a lot of attention and to feel loved, but she would be darned if she expressed this need too much for fear of "rocking the boat" and upsetting him. After a while, needy people build up so much resentment that they begin to doubt their self-worth.

Consequently, in the case of Shannon, the anger she felt eroded her self-esteem, making her clingy. She continued to ask for reassurance, but when her demands pushed others to their limits, they pushed her away, which only confirmed her thought that she was not loveable. So, she began this cycle of pouting, testing, and more clinging. The needy person is so caught up in her desire to be loved that she drowns herself in her own emotions. She is confused about what hurts are new and which ones are old. It's like a child who desires to have contact but feels undeserving to reach out to others. So, she waits for others to reach out and usually apologize; no one ever comes, and there she is, unnecessarily rejected when a few words could have prevented the suffering.

The "Needy" Person
Boundaries

The needy person has issues with maintaining realistic boundaries. This is true because realistically she would instead prefer there not be any boundaries between her and the person she truly loves. She has a wish to be close to others, even though she is aware that they have hurt her; she therefore disregards her own safety. She is hopeful that she will see a change in the other person. But this notion to "love no matter what" and at all costs is crippling, especially when it causes her to abandon the role of protector of her boundaries. Sometimes, starved by the lack of love she received growing up, she opens up to avoid not shutting out any possible source of affection. In fact, in a review of her poor boundaries, she is always willing to admit she is wrong, even if she is not, just to heal or to prevent any ripples with another person. She is little "Ms. Fix It".

The "Needy" Person
Rejection

The needy person is so sensitive to rejection and abandonment that it is everywhere she goes. She is so convinced of this that she interprets rejection, reacting to it when it is merely that the other person is not paying her enough attention. This makes her unpleasant to be with, and unfortunately, this precipitates that exact thing she fears: rejection. Something's missing or something's not right is her recurring theme. What is interesting is that the needy person is so preoccupied with loss and remains in a constant state of "mourning" that she does not realize that it hinders her therapeutic healing process, and she is unable to give a severe loss the due it deserves. When rejection does occur, she is paralyzed. Being alone is a horrible prospect, and she equates this as a punishment. This fear of rejection makes the needy person regularly test the affections or allegiances of others. However, since she questions her lovability, reassurance doesn't make her feel any better anyway. A needy person wants to be with someone right now and wants to know the other person's every move most of the time. She hates being stood up, disappointed, or ignored. So it comes as no surprise that she never indeed forgives a rejection. If she could, she wouldn't be dependent.

The "Needy" Person
Values

She values affection, consistency, and loyalty from someone who is there for her and accepts her love. She appreciates being acknowledged and remembered. But she is unforgiving to those who demonstrate the slightest bit of disloyalty. She has difficulty with this because she is very loyal herself. She is even loyal to those who don't deserve her loyalty. She values other people's company just for the sake of having company. She also involves herself with people who have little to no meaning in her life at all. The needy person is typically the a very kind hearted and loving person and loves to be around people.

For Shannon, she always needs to be with someone. She doesn't like to do anything alone and depends on other people for transportation, shopping, dining, exercising, and so on. Finding her place of solitude is not a priority. She is the original "my buddy." If you have a phone, she is the person who will be calling you when you leave, while you're on your way, and when you're pulling up. All questions about details are not questions regarding her need to control, but she needs to know if she is going to be included or not.

The "Needy" Person
The Victim

The needy person is unlikely to respond when she is faced with a hurt, and for that reason, she is more likely to become a victim. This happens because she has this crippling fear of rejection and discovering that the people who are supposed to love her do not, in fact, love her, so when she is offended or injured, she very rarely stands up for herself and instead she suffers in silence. This leads her to become trapped in situations where she can either speak up or leave. After a while, her silence leads to a storage of so much rage, hurt, and anger, which in turn causes her to doubt her self-worth. She then begins this internal debate with herself: "Am I worthy of being loved?" This is how the needy person starts to tolerate abuse because she is unwilling to take the risk that might leave her alone and lonely.

The "Needy" Person
Denial

Needy people use denial almost as their "go-to" method to deal with pain. Because of this, when a needy person is hurt, she often will not recognize or express it, leading to a built-in delay in her emotional reaction time. At times this causes her to lose touch with the things that have hurt her, and she becomes accustomed to withholding how she feels rather than be spontaneous in expressing her feelings. Typically, people do not intend to hurt one another. There are many misunderstandings that could be quickly be cleared up, but for the needy person, she lets them linger. As she pauses before expressing herself, her hurts become blown out of proportion, while the person who hurt her forgets entirely about the incident, if he or she was even aware of it in the first place. This makes reconciliation extremely difficult because the needy person is more than likely still hurt or offended and she can't seem to understand why she is holding on to the hurt. She doesn't realize it is still lingering because she never fully expressed her hurt in the moment it occurred, instead it festered.

In the case of Shannon, she would often times remain stuck on a hurt that happened years ago. The delay allows her to be dramatic and wallow in her hurt. She begins to internalize her "devastating" hurt and overstates to herself, "After all the crap he put me through, how dare he treat me like this?" Even though she keeps most of the resentment to herself, her rage is blatant, and she then distances herself from those she loves. She turns off her cell phone, she blocks phone calls, doesn't return e-mails, and secludes herself only to be a paradox. She pretends as though she wants to be alone, but is crying out for attention and to prove to herself that someone loves her.

Unfortunately, this pattern only serves to build her emotional debt and leads her to suffer. Her energy is depleted with doing this time after time, and this only makes her even more sensitive to injury. The denial she utilizes to conceal her anger only serves to exacerbate her resentment. Therefore, she remains stuck in her own emotional prison that she put herself in. I could go on, but I think you are getting the picture, so let's move on to how to deal with a needy person.

How to Engage the Needy Person

You can feel guilty for not dealing with needy people, or you can be straight with them and encourage them to stand up for themselves and to take care of themselves, knowing that their self-worth is not contingent upon someone else loving them or accepting them. The needy person needs to understand that being alone is not a complete death sentence. Actually being alone, allows you to get to know yourself in the most intimate way and if you are honest, it just may allow for growth. If you catch yourself being in a relationship, whether it be a friendship or romantic relationship, with a person who has these secondary characteristics, you need to be honest with that person. Needy people always tests limits; in other words, there are times they play games and it is to test your loyalty to them. For example, if they claim you don't care or don't love them enough, kindly validate their feelings by acknowledging them, but understand it is not feasible for you to show your love and commitment every second without pause. That's not reality. Don't be disingenuous. If you inflate how you feel, in the long run you won't be able to maintain it, you'll become bitter and resentful, and you'll pull away, telling yourself that the relationship isn't worth preserving when actually it probably was. Being honest is what's real. Operate honestly and respectfully and with care in your communication. Always show gratitude and be direct yet sensitive. I like to call it nicety (nice/nasty). Let me clarify: it's not that your directness should be offensive, but it needs to be clear and not sugar-coated. Be encouraging and remind the needy person of their worth. Stay positive.

Growth for the Needy Person

When the needy person has moved past their character flaws or has grown, they are the most pleasant person to have in your circle. For Shannon, she made an effort to grow and change the way she was processing things that happen in life. It is because of that growth she was able to relate to people honestly and openly. When the needy person has grown, she is the model for understanding, giving, showing care and concern and love. She is naturally empathetic so she has a keen sense for knowing when something is bothering someone and is the first to make herself available for you to talk to. Both her willingness to evolve and strive towards becoming a better version of herself has allowed her to be that "go to" person to talk to. She is very kind hearted, intuitive and accepting of others. There is no more evidence of her growth than to see her ability to now defend herself, know her worth and willingness to let go because she no longer equates her worth by whether someone loves her or not. She no longer looks and the mirror and questions herself because someone mistreats her.

Her relationships now are characterized by reciprocal love, warmth, sincerity, openness and appreciation. She is no longer fickled, petty and immature but rather can support her partner and be in the present with them no longer being suspect, domineering or testing. In her family, she is the glue that hold them together. She is the one who everyone wants to be around and her presence lights up the room. At work she is about her business but she is always willing to help out and speaks out against unfairness. She is very personable and every one follows her. The "evolved" needy person is the backbone of every family, relationship, workplace, team or system.

The Narcissist (Cutthroat)
Leroy

Narcissist are cutthroat—*very* cutthroat—and that is how they are defined. Take Leroy, for instance; he grew up the oldest child of three. He was more close to his grandparents than his actual parents and was therefore spoiled. He described himself as a loveable child but knew early on he would be successful. He loved to be around people and to be admired. He spoke about his relationship with his father as being abusive, and described instances where he never felt like he was good enough. As he was growing up, he felt like he always had something to prove. As he became an adult, he needed a lot of attention, feared rejection, and underneath his arrogance, he honestly had low self-esteem.

The cutthroat defense characters tend to want to be admired and viewed as successful. They exaggerate about the career accomplishments and believe they are superior. They do things to be the center of attention, and it's always a popularity contest. They are typically well liked on the surface but can be abrasive and unpleasant. Leroy wore many faces. He was also a bit of a Narcissist. He was so sick in his false reality that he couldn't see past his own bullcrap. He was prone to rebound relationships although they lasted for a while because he was so good at pulling the wool over women's eyes. His thinking was always black/white and he couldn't say anything without sarcasm. At times, he was passive aggressive. His behaviors were reminiscent of the kid in class who always had some "smart aleck" thing to say, would hit you and put you down but when the teacher caught you retaliating, he would play innocent and the teacher would believe him. But he was treacherous because he often had control issues that were subtle at first but used emotional blackmail with everyone (his girlfriend's and even his own child). His insatiable need for attention stemmed from some form of rejection he experienced. He was always full of himself, saying things like, "Yes, you can have my autograph," and he thrived on hype. He's was a legend in his world.

His behavior and mood were often dependent on and driven by feedback from his environment. For Leroy, the impression he needed to make had to be the best because he intensely guarded his self-esteem, which was a clear indication of his behavior and thoughts. He lacked empathy and was callous most times yet was sensitive; he was unappreciative and could emotionally detach quickly. In relationships, he self-sabotages but it was because he didn't have a constitution to love because he was always about self. He had a sense of entitlement always, and the opinions of others never mattered. I remember thinking in therapy that I felt sorry for his partner because he evidently lacked the ability of emotional reciprocity. The point I want to make is that his character may have been a result of his family circumstances, but his choice in defense patterns adversely affected how he engaged with the rest of the world.

<u>The Narcissist (Cutthroat)</u>
<u>Success</u>

You see, cutthroat people have talent, but they act cowardly and have very low self-esteem underneath their presentation of superior arrogance. Therefore, they seek out the things that are easy to them to achieve success in those endeavors because they can draw attention to themselves, but it does little to help them internally. Why? Because they achieve great success but at the wrong goal. A cutthroat person's drive has carried him in the wrong direction. He discovers that being at the top is about actually working and maintaining a sustained effort. However, grandiosity wins every time and most people are drawn to this type of character because they are very charming and have a winning personality up front. They also have the gift of gab. More often than not, they are in leadership positions or have their own business. You see, they are constantly seeking recognition or kudos from others to reinforce their own self-worth and they only form relationships be it professional or personal where they can see a positive reflection of themselves in the other person's eye.

The Narcissist (Cutthroat)
Character/ Ideals

"Baby, I'm a flirt." This was Leroy's nature. He was very flirtatious and engaging. He had a knack for paying attention to the person to whom he was speaking to and always made them feel as though he or she matters. He needed to feel sexually attractive, and he was always on display. His behavior was extremely infuriating to his partners, especially when his partner happened to be a controlling person who took his flirtatious nature as "out of pocket" or as rejection. Leroy hugged every woman he knew and would always flirt right in front of his girlfriends. He's is the guy who has a secret second phone that his girlfriend doesn't know about for the other women on the side. He has a secret vault of photos and text messages from the women he is creeping with on the side. He is the guy who has social media romances but is slated to be married in a few months and he's the guy where you have to watch your back because you could very well have one of his ex's confront you while you two are out on a date. He's messy. Leroy, as a cutthroat person, was a habitual line stepper. He would cross the line often and didn't like to accept correction or to be called out on his foulness. Leroy would lash out on his girlfriend if she confronted him and accuse her of the very thing he was doing thus making her question her self-worth. Leroy was slick as snot and Leroy thought he was brilliant and would tell people this. He dared to think that his brilliance and charm made up for his offensiveness and self-centeredness. The cutthroat person needs to be both applauded and the center of attention.

The Narcissist (Cutthroat)
Acting Up

One of cutthroat people's most aggravating traits is their need to "act up" rather than express their feelings openly. It's always sudden or avoidance, especially if it's too much to bear. They act out and throw tantrums just like a baby does. You see, a baby crying and kicking and falling out is no different than the adult who manipulates, pouts, and uses triangulation to get his way. It's the same concept; it just looks different in an adult. The interesting thing about cutthroat people is that they are like controlling people in that they exaggerate their needs and are dramatic. Truthfully, they find the everyday reality of a relationship tiresome and boring. For example, when Leroy couldn't handle a fight, he'd move out without notice (coward), but his texts would say, "I just need some time to be by myself," "It's not you, it's me," "I just need space," or "If you give me some time, I can be the man you need," and so on. The interesting piece to this is after his feelings of rejection and failure here, the cutthroat person simply quits his job, moves away, starts a new career, or finds a new lover—and if he is really dealing in pathology, he will start a whole new family and try to live a double life. On the surface, none of the things appear to be irrational, but merely a logical response to the stimulus.

Let me break this down even further. Acting out makes it extremely difficult to identify the cutthroat person because he changes identities frequently. He changes attitudes, his circle of friends, hobbies, and even his belief systems. Running away never solves cutthroat people's problems, and yet they seem to think if they create a new environment that their temporary fake happiness will last long, and then they are puzzled about why they keep being miserable after short periods of time. The truth of the matter is that their endeavors may be new and something different, but they always help them avoid their lack of belief in their self-worth and self-esteem. Therefore, if left unchecked, these people live a life unfulfilled because they will always be searching for something new to make them feel good but not having an accurate understanding of why they keep repeating patterns of behavior that prove to be harmful to them and the others in their lives. If not careful, the cutthroat person can be very toxic.

If I had words of wisdom, they would be: don't build your identity behind your deficits/defenses. If you're always defensive, you can't grow, and will remain stagnant in all areas of your life. You will recognize this if you are a person who says things like, "That's just me, I'm me." Truthfully, for some of us, we wouldn't even know who we'd be if we had to let go of the pain, hang-ups, and our ways.

7 EMOTIONAL PRISON

The nucleus of all emotional problems stems from pain not being addressed in its immediacy. It is when you pause in expressing your emotion that the emotion is stored rather than expressed. You often block out pain because you can't face the reality of it or its consequences. As a result, hurt converts to anger and guilt, and anxiety turns to rage. All of these emotions are stored in what I call an emotional prison. Denial causes you to be unaware of your hurt, creating a state of shock that ranges from confusion before you realize someone has hurt your feelings to forgetting what trauma just occurred. You implement defenses to justify your rage or to make others seem at fault for your problems. You pretend not to care to save face, but all of these defenses create an emotional prison.

Existing in Emotional Prison

Living in the state of an emotional prison has to do with unexpressed feelings of the present or the past few days or weeks. Usually, these unexpressed emotions are the reaction to the event that just has happened or is still evolving, and you haven't gotten your mind wrapped around it yet. Typically, you're keenly aware that you're hurting and of the reasons why you spend a significant amount of the time of your life in the current emotional prison waiting for the opportunity to speak your mind or for some release. Someone steps on your toes or hurt your feelings for one reason or another, and you're unable to express yourself immediately, or you're faced with the threat. You're trying to figure out in your head how are you going to respond, and in either case, your emotion is immediate, but your responses to it are delayed.

Holding Back

There is a storage war room of feelings, and this occurs because at the moment that you feel something it's either awkward to express it or you just plain don't feel like opening up. Truthfully, there are situations where in the present they may not offer you an opportunity to show your feelings appropriately. It may be a work situation where expressing your feelings would be considered unbusinesslike and unprofessional or even a social position where you may be deemed uncouth. The circumstances may be uncertain, so communicating your emotional reaction might be jumping to a questionable conclusion. However, what I can tell you is that you if you have unresolved emotions with a person who just hurt you, you may shy away from expressing yourself because you don't want to start something bigger or you don't want to react in such a way that is permanently damaging. But I will say that does take maturity. When you're emotionally mature, more often than not you don't allow someone to disturb your peace or steal your joy, so the words of a fool, an emotionally troubled person, or somebody who is viciously attacking you may be sent to throw you off guard, but you won't respond to them. Nevertheless, there is still an emotion being felt that has not been acknowledged.

Managing

In life you will continually experience heartache, pains, stress, and disappointment; they all add to your emotional prison. But it is vital to develop an attitude that allows you to adapt to frustration without responding automatically and becoming enraged. You saw that the objective is to be aware but disenthralled, present but distant, caring but nonchalant, responsive but not drawn into the drama. You manage standards every day and respond best by assuming the viewpoint of detachment. In other words, pick your battles. Don't let unimportant things upset you. Do the best you can with what you have and accept the things that you cannot change. Conversely, when you are an emotional prison, you find it problematic—almost impossible—to be dispassionate because you have stored feelings that are always looking for a release and they tend to attach themselves to everyday disappointments. Your emotional prison interferes with the way feelings naturally extinguish and eventually fade away. The purpose of processing feelings efficiently is to reduce the muck of submerged feelings that a person who is hurt doesn't call for. This causes the agitation period when it comes to feelings, and remembering what is important and needs to be expressed while letting go of what is not is a lifelong lesson.

Holding On to Hurt and Rage

We have all experienced things that has taking us to a whole other level of hurt and behind that hurt develops rage depending on the offense. I will go as far as to say that we've all have experienced hurt so severe that it may have very well landed us on an episode of *SNAPPED*. The pain of heartache, betrayal or abuse is all too real. However, understand that it is self-abuse when you replay over and repeatedly the hurt you've endured and decide to remain stuck there. It may be one thing to think about what occurred in the past and understand it, learn from it, and grow, but staying stuck in that kind of toxicity is another thing you don't need. When you're in the emotional prison state, you are trying to figure out or decide how you should react, or maybe you're waiting for the courage or the opportunity to tell someone how you feel. In a sense, most of us are doing our bid and trying to get out of emotional prison. You're trying to make sense of your emotions and your feelings, you try to figure out how someone could treat you so poorly, and if you were hurt—and if so, what you are going to do about it. Like everyone else, you're a prisoner of your insecurity, and you fear rejection and being vulnerable.

Anxiety/Worry

Growing up I would hear that it's a sin to worry, and while I believe in the word that it's true, the fact remains that worry is a worthy topic because it wreaks havoc on people's lives. Anxiety is often labeled as something else. You see, the fear of rejection produces anxiety. Stress happens when the hurt is stored but hasn't occurred yet; this happens because you imagine things that could happen. Your purpose in holding anxiety in the current emotional prison is to establish a state of caution and maintain your awareness until the present danger is over.

Let's break it down. In confronting physical danger, you want to be strong and fast. You set your anxiety aside so you can concentrate on survival mode without thinking about it. However, you cannot solve a difficult problem without using your mind. You can't use your mind if you can't seem to concentrate. When facing something like a mental challenge, obsessing about the threat or trying not to think about it both limit your ability to feel the same defenses that allow you to store anxiety. They also limit your ability to think clearly Things that are held in your emotional prison activate your self-doubts, which allow you to slow down and get in your mind's way if that makes sense instead of focusing on the problem that needs your attention. You become preoccupied with questions regarding your worth, your intelligence, your goodness and your self-worth. Every challenge becomes a test of your self-esteem when anxiety can run amok. You panic. You cannot think. It is important to note that anxiety is stored in any situation where there is prolonged exposure to uncertainty or risk, such as being in an unhealthy relationship where your partner continually threatens to break up with you or the manager you're working for is unstable and threatens to fire you. Unreleased anxiety defeats your defenses' ability to contain it, so it intrudes and interferes with your life. You become increasingly restless and are easily irritated and distracted. The most compromising experiences are those where anxiety is relentless, real, and oppressive, and the means to deal with it is limited. In such situations of that emotional prison, it overwhelms and completely distorts your perception.

Not Letting Go of Resentment

There is always some old hurt that goes unmourned.

Holding on to resentment can give you a slow death, and you may not even be aware of it. Your emotional prison can sometimes include hurt and resentment, and when these two are put together, it's usually because at the time you were unable to speak up about something, or quite frankly, you have low self-esteem and you fear rejection. Nonetheless, don't be fooled, because it is this paralyzing fear of rejection that causes you to be focused on something tangible, and by doing this you feel like you are able to manage your life. You feel like it's under control, but of course, the thing that you are trying to control eventually starts to control you, as all stored feelings do. Your fear begins to paralyze you.

If you fear rejection, naming the person you are angry with can be dreadful. Remember Lamar who developed anxiety or the case of the cowardly lion every time he would get into arguments with his partners. He found it difficult to admit he was angry and express himself appropriately. He had an even more significant issue with accepting he was wrong and humbling himself instead he would either run away or project his ill behavior on to someone else. He was very egotistical and emotionally immature. Only after he could admit that his first wife hurt him could he allow himself to express anger. Instead he kept it in and lashed out in subsequent relationships. Every woman he encountered after his first wife, paid for his inability to heal from that past hurt. If Lamar could've realized and admitted his hurt and devastation, his symptoms would begin to dissipate, and he would be able to have semi-healthy relationships. He could've loved and received love again. But Lamar never realized he was still stuck. In the meantime, he continued to go on hurting women and abusing them both mentally and emotionally, ripping their heart out. He could go on with plenty of women year after year but he will never truly be happy because he never got to the nucleus of how to heal. Although not cured of his maladaptive behaviors, identifying the foundation of his hurt would be a critical point in his healing process. However, to most, when you are hurting, you feel justified in your anger. But admitting your hurt allows you to direct the anger at the correct source without feeling guilty. Not identifying the hurt or acknowledging your hurt or living in denial makes you feel bad; like a person who is angry for no good reason. You remain emotionally stunted, and if not careful, you become numb and don't feel. This is very dangerous because you can develop what some call a "black heart" unable to feel empathy or being cold and callous. The inability to feel allows you to hurt people and not feel one ounce of remorse. It allows you to continue on the pattern of hurting others and having the audacity to believe they should just get over it. When you don't have the capacity to feel for others at some point you will feel the same misery you brought onto others.

Consequently, not being able to identify the source of your hurt also leads to misdirected anger, acting out, and hurting others repeatedly. Hurt people hurt people. In case of both Lamar and Leroy, they were emotionally inept and incredibly immature. They were not able to take responsibility for their feelings and their life, and therefore their healing hadn't even begun. Both could tell themselves all day long that they were happy and move on to the next dysfunction, but they had repeated patterns of dysfunction. For Lamar, time and time again, he failed to understand how his immaturity, selfishness and the irresponsibility of his feelings didn't allow for the natural healing process. No matter how much Lamar might have felt that he was hurt, it was his job to speak up, and to do this, he needed to believe in himself. Otherwise he would risk losing himself and not knowing who he would become in subsequent relationships, which was a deceitful callous monster.

Sometimes it takes a lot of pain for a person to get to that place. No matter how badly someone hurts you, the responsibility lies with you to stand up and defend yourself. The truth is that when you think about old hurts, you often wish that you had put up a fight or told someone about themselves, although I might add the caveat that that's not the Christian thing to do. However, when memories of a painful event surface months or even years later, you're likely to obsess over your passivity because old hurts will haunt you until you decide to take responsibility for acting on them, even if you were innocent. It's wise to take responsibility for some part of the damage that was done to you, not to excuse the other person but to reclaim your power. If you can accept that there was something you could have done to protect yourself, you can believe that you still have the power now to defend yourself from future hurts. Taking back power allows you to give up on your investment of being a victim, and you can heal.

Even though you may try to be honest and face your hurts and express your emotions as they occur, there is always some old hurt that goes unmourned. Don't permit yourself to get lost in rage or tears of pure frustration. Instead, pay close attention to the unexplainable part of your response. Accept that your old feelings have just been activated and see this invasion as a privilege. Be grateful for the opportunity to heal this intrusion, and consider what has happened and how you reacted. But you need to ask yourself if there is an abundance of frustration in these feelings that you're expressing? This is a tough thing to admit, since like everyone else, you want to think of yourself as a well-balanced person. Remember that this is an exercise in deciphering things that led you to distorting the truth. Be patient and open to the possibility that you're not perfect, and that's a fact! Your imperfection is a reality that you'll have to face, but on the flip side, this may help you discover some new strength about yourself. The ultimate goal of healing old hurt is to understand what happened and not allow yourself to get lost in the past pain. Don't sidestep your feelings because they're uncomfortable for you. *Get comfortable with being uncomfortable.*

We're all here on this earth to give a gift. You deserve to live a life that is free from emotional jail as much as you possibly can. If you can live emotionally debt-free, then you can spend your energy pursuing your life's purpose and maintaining balance. Truthfully, when you bury your past, you risk losing wisdom that was gained from learning from your mistakes. When you conceal your sorrow, you also hide your love. You need to be truthful about the past and allow the natural therapeutic process to take place. You're only a prisoner of the things that you cannot accept, so take your bid and get out of emotional prison.

8 HURTING BUT HEALING

The Lord is close to the broken hearted and saves those who are crushed in spirit. ~ Psalm 34:18

If you don't profess it, you cannot address it. Repairing the previous damage done to you is not just about your need to be better but is a result of your commitment to be vulnerable, to accept that you cannot change the past, to accept your imperfections, and to take responsibility for the role you may have played in how your life is turning out. Letting go of hurt you have stored and emotional baggage is a necessary step in healing. Releasing hurt is an essential factor of forgiving because you release others and you release yourself. Forgiveness is not possible unless you are willing to change and grow. Admit your weaknesses and accept them as part of yourself. Your ability to be taking care of yourself determines how quickly you deal with the pain of your life. I am not asserting that it is easy but understand that you cannot let it control your life.

The moment you cannot be free, there's a problem. You have to come to accept the reality of your past wombs which many consist of someone who has hurt you, abandoned you, betrayed you, cheated on you or abused you. Somebody didn't love you the way that you thought you should be loved, or they left you, or you weren't cherished for the person you are; all these things you may have experienced, but you need to understand what happened to you. You compromised. You gave in to the belief that you were less and took the path betraying yourself, and you did so by holding grudges and acting in anger. You sought revenge, and you denied your hurt, and you allowed your rage to grow out of control, even hurting others the way that they hurt you. But your recognition of these unresolved pains is another opportunity for you to correct these imbalances. You can never go back to the past and relive it, so for example, understand that you need to accept that you can never make someone who does not love you already love you. Let me repeat: you cannot make people love you. They will only love you as much as they love themselves. Let me break that last statement down. People who intentionally or who selfishly hurt others or who use or abuse others cannot love themselves. Take the guy who deserts his child to go live his life and or has multiple children everywhere, nine times out of ten, his irresponsibility, abandonment, and selfishness is a result of some form of his past hurt and rejection he experienced himself. Both in his folly and selfishness, he doesn't realize his children are half of him. Let me go deep for moment. Some parents have a negative self-worth which sometimes is disguised as arrogance. But it is their negative self-image in which they inadvertently extend to their children. If a father or mother cannot love themselves, and extend this negativity to their offspring, then it is not surprising that they cannot pass love and tenderness to what they have created. Additionally, some parents who are immature and selfish view their children as an unwanted, dependent burden. Hence you have the father who abandons their child or children. How can a man—or should I say "male"—abuse part of him by showing no care or concern for what he created? One can only surmise that he doesn't truly love himself or know what the essence of true love is. Make sense?

You need to accept that you have no control over others. Heck, you barely have control over the events of your life, so you need to let go of others and release them to their destinies and you to yours. You can live in this world for many years, and trust me, you won't be able to please everybody. But you need to reach your stars and find victory on your terms, and you can't do that if you have emotional baggage. Understand that enjoying the good things in life is merely impossible if you can't come to terms with the truth and let go.

9 FORGIVENESS

Whether your incentive is spiritual, religious, moral, or psychological, the fundamental goal is forgiveness. For me, forgiveness is necessary, and if I don't forgive, I have an automatic problem with God because he calls us to forgive. There's no wheeling and dealing with this. If you identify yourself as a person who lives by Godly principles, know that forgiveness is not an optional part of your life. It is an essential part of what it means to be a Christian. If we are going to follow Jesus, we must forgive. We have no other choice. We must forgive as God has forgiven us—completely, freely, and graciously. To me, the best incentive to forgiving someone is to simply remember how much God forgave me. You have to understand that forgiveness breaks the cycle of resentment and bitterness that entraps you with pain. You can forgive people if they don't ask for forgiveness. You can forgive without restoring the relationship. If you're a Christian, then examine forgiveness like this: it is a gift given freely just like salvation. It cannot be earned.

Now let's be clear that time does not heal all wounds; it only allows rage and resentment to fester. True forgiveness is such hard work. Let me repeat true forgiveness is very difficult. However, forgiveness is not forgetting. I always say that in life, there are choices, and forgiveness is a choice. It is a crisis of the will. Forgiveness is agreeing to live with the consequences of another's sin. It is giving up anger and resentment that you may be entitled to and giving the offender a gift that he or she is not. Forgiveness is costly because you pay the price for the evil you forgive.

There is no way to talk about emotional healing, resilience, or dealing with any hurt without talking about the concept of forgiveness. Many of you will say that you have a hard time forgiving, that you don't forgive, that you get even, or that you struggle. I think it's safe to say that no one wants to be offended. However, I'd be remiss if I didn't say that the reason why so many of us struggle is that we simply don't honestly know what forgiveness is about. Let's examine, shall we?

To begin to think about forgiving someone who has hurt you intentionally or inadvertently, you need to understand what real forgiveness is really about. It is not forgetting, condoning, or excusing the offense. It is not stating that there will be no consequences or that you cannot feel angry about being hurt or offended. Additionally, it isn't about the offender coming to you and admitting he or she was wrong or even making a promise to change the way he or she treats you. Although many of us want someone to be able to admit that they were wrong and that they have hurt us. But what happens when that never comes? You remain stuck and angry and the chances of repairing that relationship is slim to none. In some cases, the loss of restoration of a relationship may be alright but it doesn't stop the offended from still wallowing in hurt which as I stated earlier, will adversely affect one's ability to move forward in a healthy manner. The real issue is that if you don't forgive, you give that person the power to control how you feel and sometimes how you respond. You give away your power to heal, move on, and grow. Do not give away the power of your own emotions. If you are a person who likes a lot of attention and wants to play the victim, then its easier to understand why you won't forgive, but you're fooling yourself if you think you will have inner peace. That offense that you are choosing not to forgive will rear its ugly head again and again. Forgiveness is a process. Let's explore phases of forgiveness.

My senior year in undergraduate school, I studied the concept of forgiveness because it had to do with my senior thesis. I had no idea how profound that research would be to me almost fifteen years later. Psychologist, Robert Enright discussed forgiveness and broke it down into four phases: the uncovering phase, decision phase, work phase, and deepening phase.

During the uncovering phase, you come to terms with how deeply you've been hurt. This is when you get in touch with the rawness of your emotions and the hatred, anger, rage, or disgust surfaces. You gain insight into the offense, you struggle to figure out how you're going to function, and you determine how much energy you will spend on this. The good thing is now that you are aware, you can begin to heal. The decision phase is where you understand that you've been hurt, but you know that you must begin to process and shift focus so you can continue with the healing process. It is during this time that you may experience a "change of heart" and realize that you are going to move in the positive direction and make a choice to forgive the person who offended you. During the work phase, you have to do the work. This is where you try to make sense of the reason why that person may have hurt you and who that person is. I always used to say, "deal with people in their context." During this phase, you recognize that the offender isn't the devil and begin to feel empathy toward the offender. This phase may take some time. Perhaps a long time. Remember that forgiveness isn't for the offender; often, it is for yourself.

Lastly, the deepening phase is where you have what I call an "epiphany." You are releasing that emotional baggage of unforgiveness and getting out of emotional debt. The newfound meaning you get leads to increased compassion for others and yourself. Now that we have covered phases, let's examine its power.

The Power of Forgiveness

For if you forgive men their trespasses, your heavenly Father will also forgive you. But if you do not forgive men their trespasses, neither will your Father forgive your trespasses.
~Matthew 6:15

Forgiveness is very powerful. You see, you cannot heal negative emotions and actions with another negative action. Two negatives don't make a positive. We all could trade war stories about how someone betrayed us and did us wrong and doesn't deserve forgiveness in our eyes. But the truth of the matter is that everyone is worthy of forgiveness because we are all sinful people. I realize that last statement is controversial, and many of you reading this are turning your faces up at this. While I don't mean to be preachy about forgiveness, let me share what has been helpful for me. Often, we become so angry at ourselves for something we did or allowed to happen that we forget that we need to forgive ourselves.

For me, forgiving myself was crucial, because I didn't want to remain stuck and keep replaying the trauma that I had experienced, but more importantly, I needed to let go of what I was holding against myself so that I could move on with God. Psalm 66:18 states, "If I had cherished sin in my heart, the Lord would not have listened." I didn't want anything hindering my prayers and hindering me moving in the direction God had set for my life. My relationship with him is more essential and more valuable then clinging to the emotions of anger, rage, hurt, and bitterness—the very emotions that can destroy you. For me, I knew that rehearsing the scenes of the offenses done to me was in direct contrast to the Word of God (Phil. 4:9), which states to dwell on things that are true, noble, right, pure, and admirable. It takes so much energy to be angry, hateful, and resentful, so I had to take action and not expend any more energy on those things. Now, I will be very honest and say, it was and is hard work. It was daily even hourly prayers and encouragement that I had to do in order to get there. It wasn't easy. However, how dare I desire to be forgiven and not forgive others who have offended me? I had to be humble.

Lastly, as a therapist, it is important to practice what you preach. Forgiving myself was important because of the influence I have on others. People who are hurting, nine out of ten times have hurt others. I understood that I didn't deserve to suffer anymore, and I didn't want to have misdirected anger for whatever happened to me. While I can't change all the wrong that's happened, I realize that I could redirect my energy by helping others, ministering to others, and empowering them to be their best selves. At the end of the day, you're going to live with those consequences whether you chose to forgive or not.

10 SKILLS TO HEAL

When something in us is disowned, it wreaks havoc on us.
~Ralph H. Blum & Susan Coughlan

Carrying on emotional baggage has stunted your growth, emotionally, spiritually, mentally, and even physically. In fact, studies have shown that suppressing emotions uses a considerable amount of energy and robs your body of the energy that should be used for vital functions. Researchers purport that negative emotions tax our spleen, liver, adrenal glands, and use up nutrients the body needs to sustain itself. The result is fatigue, autoimmune disorders (i.e., Graves' disease, Crohn's disease, Lupus, Type 1 Diabetes), and lowered vitality. Carrying around emotional baggage is similar to carrying a ten-pound bag of sand. Imagine carrying that load wherever you go; in the shower, to work, to class, every time you get into your car, when you go to the bathroom. It would be a heavy load. You start to feel tired all the time and dread doing anything. It would begin to disrupt your ability to sleep, enjoy everyday tasks, think clearly, and concentrate. Everything around you starts to suffer, and you begin to use your defenses to help you navigate the world of emotional garbage you are hanging on to.

The fact of the matter is that the more you hang on to painful memories, old offenses, and so on, the more tired and despondent you will become. However, understand that you to do not have to remain stuck. You are under no obligation to allow anything or anyone—not even yourself—to "mess with your peace." Your peace is necessary, just like food and water, and the sooner you realize that, you will begin to let go of things and people who threaten it.

We all possess the capability to heal ourselves. Whether we have tapped into our strengths, acknowledge God's ability to heal our hearts, or become aware of our abilities is another thing. Starting right now, I implore you to take the initiative to do the necessary work it takes to live a life that is free from past wounds, bitterness, emptiness, unforgiveness, hatred, anger, and resentment. Decide to live an emotionally debt-free life. While not exhaustive, I'd like to share what has kept me out of emotional prison. I had to commit to not allowing negative emotions to have power over me or my life, and you need to make that choice to commit to living freely too.

Remember, commitment is doing what you said you would do long after the moment in which you said it in has passed. Commitment is not just saying you will do something because it feels right at the moment. Now that you have finished the book, you may feel empowered, inspired, and ready to make changes. That's magnificent, but commit to living your life free from an emotional prison.

NIA'S STEPS

1. **Develop and Use a Moral Compass:** Your moral compass is your core values. As you were growing up as a child, you were taught right from wrong, and this is an ongoing life lesson. Do not mistreat people and expect to be treated well. Do not sow a negative seed. You know to treat others with respect, honesty, empathy and compassion. Hopefully, you know to possess these ethics, and with that, you develop a conscience that should serve as your internal moral compass. If you have a moral compass, you can enact and model ethical behavior. This allows you to make decisions about your life and how you will engage with others in the world. You know how to treat someone well, and you know what behaviors to accept. Keeping your own "ground rules" for how you will treat others and allow others to treat you will keep you in less emotional turmoil.

2. **Develop Spirituality/Prayer:** From early on as a child, I was taught to place God first in my life. How does this relate to my ability to be emotionally debt-free? For me, prayer is something I get to do. Prayer allows me to commune with God; it will enable me to praise him and worship him for my life. I am reminded of his love like no other. It has been able to give me peace of mind by trusting in his word and allowing him to do work in my life. Daily I seek him, but in my times of need, I could lay all my burdens at his feet and have his will done in my life. This takes practice, but it is very possible.

3. **Change Your Perception:** When someone says or does something to offend you or hurt your feelings, know that that is one person's perception of you. It is not gospel, nor is it *your*

DEFENSES: GETTING OUT OF EMOTIONAL PRISON

truth. Does it hurt? Of course, because it is in direct contrast to what you may think about yourself. Don't let someone else's ill treatment of you become your value.

4. **Journaling:** Journaling can be very cathartic. When you journal, you are reflecting on your feelings. Most times it provides a sense of clarity both mentally and emotionally. You validate what you've experienced and come to understand that experience and yourself. Journaling also aids in emotional intelligence, which is the ability to perceive and manage your emotions and those of others. Journaling is an outlet for processing emotions and increases self-awareness. This intimate familiarity becomes a bridge of empathy; you'll better intuit and understand what others are experiencing. Most times journaling brings your emotions and motivation into alignment with your values.

5. **Find a Supportive Friend or Group:** Sharing experiences and finding better ways to cope are sometimes benefits of having a support group or friend who understands the trials and tribulations you go through. I am not saying go to them for advice, but we often need to vent and know that we are being heard because that allows our feelings to be validated. Understand that if you keep on repeating the same patterns of behaviors and unhealthy thoughts, then you're stuck in the cycle because you're applying the same logic, which is yielding the same results. It's OK to admit that some of your problems are gigantic and you could use an accountability partner who will support you, encourage you, and not let you remain stuck in the trenches with emotional baggage. Understand that your life is shaped by your thoughts. Be very picky about what thoughts you entertain or what negative people you allow into your life. Both disturb your peace and don't provide the opportunity for you to heal.

Peace of mind is so necessary, and to achieve it, you need to accept that you are the one who is capable of loving you the best. In other words, you need to accept yourself and live in truth. Defense mechanisms don't provide permanent protection from life's pain. The more we lie to ourselves, the more misery we bring. If you don't profess it, you can't address it. That's why it is so crucial that we live in consistent truth. When you accept responsibility for your life, you can view that you are a work in progress. I love the saying, "Don't judge me; God isn't through with me yet," because it is genuine. Remember, do not let anyone mess with your peace. Don't stay in emotional prison. You've done your bid, now go and live free.

REFERENCES

Blum, R. H., & Loughan, S. (1995). The healing runes: Tools for the recovery of body, mind, heart and soul. New York, NY: St. Martin's Press

Cramer, P. (1991a). The development of defense mechanisms: Theory, research and assessment. New York: Springer-Verlag.

Cramer, P. (2004). Identity change in adulthood: The contribution of defense mechanisms and life experiences. Journal of Research in Personality, 38, 280–316.

Enright, R. D., & Fitzgibbons, R. P. (2001). Forgiveness in psychotherapy: An overview. Helping clients forgive: empirical guide for resolving anger and restoring hope, 13-27. doi:10.1037/10381-001 web-site: www.forgiveness-institute.org.

Enright, R. D. (2012). The forgiving life: A pathway to overcoming resentment and creating a legacy of love. (APA Lifetools). Washington, DC: American What's the Difference Between a Feeling and an Emotion? (2014, December 19). Retrieved from https://www.psychologytoday.com/us/blog/hide-and-seek/201412/whats-the-difference-between feeling-and-emotion

Weinstock, A. R. (1967). Family environment and the development of defense and coping mechanisms. Journal of Personality and Social Psychology, 5(1), 67-75. http://dx.doi.org/10.1037/h0024194

www.ingramcontent.com/pod-product-compliance
Lightning Source LLC
LaVergne TN
LVHW091319080426
835510LV00007B/565